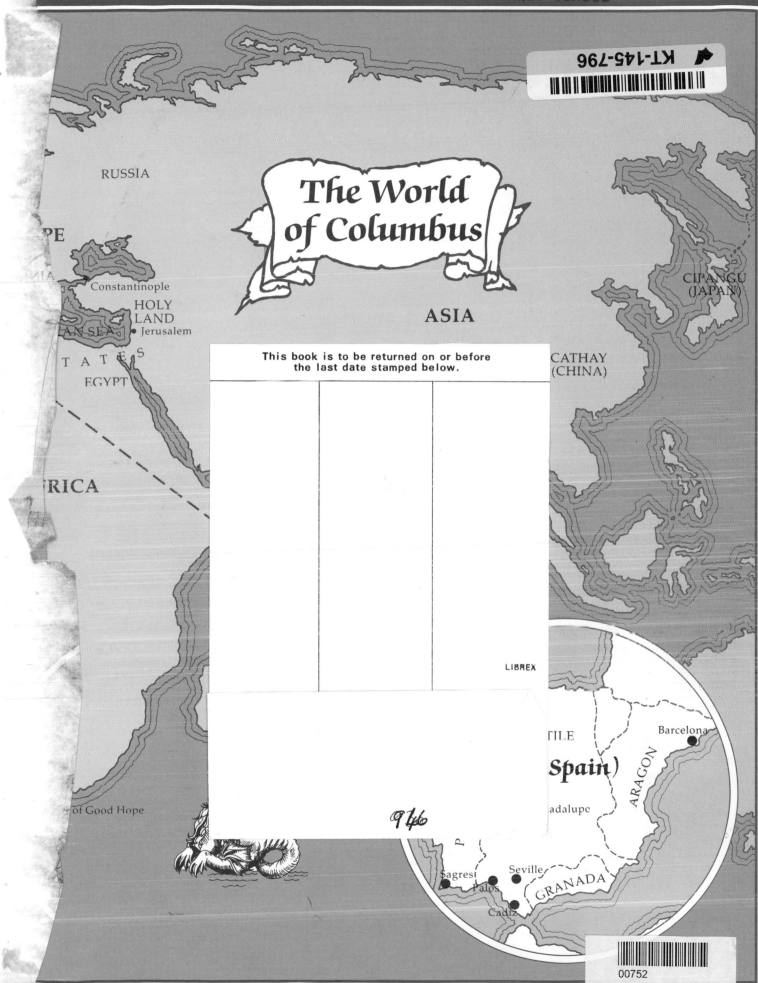

RUSSIA

The World of Columbus

Constantinople

HOLY
LAND

Jerusalem

ASIA

EGYPT

CIPANGU
(JAPAN)

CATHAY
(CHINA)

FRICA

TILE

Barcelona

Spain)

ARAGON

adalupe

of Good Hope

946

Sagres

Seville

Palos

GRANADA

Cadiz

752

I WAS THERE
CHRISTOPHER
COLUMBUS

I WAS THERE

CHRISTOPHER COLUMBUS

JOHN D. CLARE

Consultant Editor BARRY IFE

THE BODLEY HEAD
LONDON

First published in Great Britain in 1992
by The Bodley Head Children's Books,
an imprint of The Random Century Group Ltd
20 Vauxhall Bridge Road, London SW1V 2SA

Random Century Australia Pty Ltd
20 Alfred Street, Sydney, NSW 2061

Random Century New Zealand Ltd
PO Box 40-086, Glenfield, Auckland 10, New Zealand

Random Century South Africa Pty Ltd
PO Box 337, Bergvlei 2012, South Africa

ISBN   0-370-31650-9

A CIP catalogue record for this book is available from
the British Library

Created and produced by Roxby Paintbox Co. Ltd
126 Victoria Rise, London SW4 0NW

Director of Photography Tymn Lyntell
Photography Charles Best
Art Director Dalia Hartman
Production Manager Fiona Nicholson
Book Production Manager Avril Litchmore

Editor Gilly Abrahams
Series Editor Susan Elwes
Co-ordinating Editor Laura Ward
Map/Time-line Simon Ray-Hills
Picture Research Lesley Coleman
Typesetting Sue Estermann

Reproduction Catalyst Repro Technology; Columbia
Offset Ltd; Trademasters Ltd

Printed in Hong Kong

ACKNOWLEDGEMENTS

Make-up: Alex Cawdron, Pam Foster, Stella Jacobs. Set de-
sign and building: Art FX Associates, John Preston. Casting:
Baba Rodgers. Photographer's assistants: Michael Harvey,
Nicola Moyes. Location management (Spain): Jacqueline
Moya Dixon. Replica Columbus boats: Sociedad Estatal
Quinto Centenario. Christopher Columbus portrayed by
Manolo Santos.

Roxby Paintbox would also like to thank: Kathryn Steele-
Child and Ron White at Bermans International; John
Brumfit Cigar Merchants; Cocoa Council; Cotton Council
International; Caroline and Dante Concha; M. C. Creative
Ltd; R. and S. Dent; Farley Hire Ltd; J. B. Gates; Martin Gee;
Cecelia Herrera; The International Sailing Craft Association;
Keely Hire Ltd; The Kentwell Tudor Pavilion made by Past
Tents, Notts; Roy King; National Maritime Museum, Green-
wich; Lewis and Kaye Ltd; London Docklands Development
Corporation Ltd; Arthur Middleton Antique Scientific In-
struments; Rentabook Ltd; Ken Paul Ltd; Rita and Lolita
Catering; Roadrunner Film Services; Trading Post Ltd;
Scheduled Air; Southern Film Services; Square Sail Shipyard;
St Mary's Church, Clapham; Harriet Wynter Arts & Sciences.

Additional photographs: Ajax News and Feature Service,
pp32-3; reproduced by permission of the British Library,
p8, 63 top left; Fotomas Index, p43; Hereford Cathedral,
p6 bottom left; Mansell Collection, p63 bottom right; Mary
Evans Picture Library, p32; Scala/Museo Navale di Pegli,
p62; National Maritime Museum, pp44-5; Sonia Halliday
and Laura Lushington Photographs, p7 bottom left; Susan
Griggs Agency, pp26-7.

Contents

The World of Columbus

Christopher Columbus is one of the most famous explorers in history. He is remembered – some say wrongly – as the man who discovered America.

He was born halfway through the fifteenth century, during the time known as the Middle Ages – the age of knights, castles, tournaments and courtly love. The Hundred Years War was not yet finished, and the Battle of Agincourt (1415) was still within living memory. Joan of Arc had been burned at the stake only 20 years earlier.

Medieval scholars knew little about science or geography. The fourteenth-century writer Nicole Oresme had realized that 'the earth is round like a ball', but even he believed that 'the earth is at the centre of the universe'. The *mappae mundi* (maps drawn up by the Christian Church) still showed a flat earth

with Jerusalem at the centre. Ideas about geography had not changed much since the time of the Greek writer Ptolemy, who lived in the second century AD.

Europeans such as Marco Polo had travelled into Asia and Africa but their books, copied laboriously by hand, often mixed fact with fantasy. It was believed that parts of the Ocean Sea (the Atlantic) were so hot that the water boiled, and the tides so strong that a ship which sailed there would never return. An English traveller, Sir John Mandeville, claimed to have seen the Earthly Paradise – the Garden of Eden – surrounded by mountains, deserts and rushing rivers. Other tales told of Prester John, a Christian king living somewhere in Africa, who had great wealth and invincible armies. The Church argued that if antipodes (people who lived on the other side of the world) existed, they must be the devil's creation, or else they would fall off into space. Writers described man-creatures with ears like elephants, or faces on their chests; others were said to have one huge

foot which they held up like an umbrella when it rained. Ordinary people could not check whether these stories were true or false but they chose to believe them.

In 1492 nobody in Europe knew of the existence of the American continent. Scholars thought that to the west, between Europe and Cathay (China), lay one huge ocean in which, perhaps, were some large islands called Brazil, Antilia and Cipangu (Japan).

Yet only 70 years later an Italian called the century after 1450 the Renaissance, meaning rebirth. It seemed to him that, after centuries of stagnation, there was progress once again. 'The world sailed around, America discovered, the compass invented, the printing press sowing knowledge, ancient manuscripts rescued and learning restored,' boasted a French writer, 'all witness the triumph of our New Age.' Columbus, the 'discoverer of America', had played a major part in bringing about this new age.

Christians and Muslims

In Renaissance times, although several remarkable women achieved great things, men dominated every area of public life. Women usually cared for the children and managed the house and farmwork, while their husbands ran the government, fought their wars, traded and travelled. Renaissance men were often violent and arrogant. They believed that if they worked hard they could become rich and famous, and change the world.

Most Europeans were Christian. People of other religions were considered to be heathens who ought to be conquered and converted to Christianity. During the fifteenth century, however, the Christian countries of Europe suffered several defeats. Jerusalem and the Holy Land were already in Muslim hands. In 1453 the Turks, who were Muslims, captured Constantinople (Istanbul). In 1480 they captured the port of Otranto in Italy and set up

a market where they sold Christian slaves. Only the Christian rulers of Castile and Aragon in Spain – at that time divided into a number of states – were able to gain any victories in their war against the Muslim kingdom of Granada.

In the Middle Ages the countries of western Europe imported silk and spices from the East. Silk was a luxury, but spices were essential to disguise the taste of bad meat and rotten vegetables – it was not yet known how to keep food fresh. By conquering the entire eastern Mediterranean, the Muslims cut Europe off from trade with India and China.

Some Europeans tried to find alternative trade routes to India. The rulers of Portugal, for example, encouraged voyages of exploration around the south of Africa. They also hoped to discover the kingdom of Prester John, so they could make an alliance with him against the Muslims.

Columbus's voyage to America was undertaken to try to discover yet another way to India and the East – by sailing west, across the Ocean Sea.

The New World

Columbus was not the first person to reach America. In prehistoric times tribesmen from Asia made their way into the continent, probably through Alaska. The twentieth-century adventurer Thor Heyerdahl sailed a papyrus boat across the Atlantic to prove that the ancient Egyptians could have discovered America. An inscription, supposedly 2,500 years old, was discovered in Brazil in 1872. 'We came from the Red Sea around [Africa] but were separated by a storm,' it reads, 'so we have come here, twelve men and three women.' Although it was dismissed as a fake because of mistakes in its grammar, scholars have since discovered ancient texts from the Middle East written in exactly the same style. Archaeologists have proved with absolute certainty that, in about AD 1000, the Vikings settled in Newfoundland and traded with the natives.

During the 1470s and 1480s the Portuguese made a number of attempts to cross the Atlantic, and Danish fishermen sailed beyond Iceland towards Greenland and Labrador. At about the same time English explorers set out from the port of Bristol to look for the 'Isle of Brasil'. Some historians claim that the English reached Newfoundland in 1481, but kept their discovery a secret while they fished there for cod.

Genoa

It is almost certain that Cristoforo Colombo (Columbus) was born in Genoa in 1451. His father, Domenico, was a wool weaver and his sister married a cheesemonger, yet Columbus became one of the most famous explorers the world has ever known.

In the fifteenth century Italy was divided into a number of small states. The city-state of Genoa was one of the greatest cities of the age. More than 5,000 houses, each five or six storeys high, were packed into half a square mile (130 hectares). Outside the city walls there were about 2,000 houses, including the mansions of the nobility and wealthy merchants.

Genoa was a prosperous trading centre, where French, German, English, Spanish, Portuguese, Jewish and Arab traders haggled over goods brought from the East by Genoese merchants. On sale were pepper, ginger and sugar (used as a medicine, not as a sweetener); wool, cotton and silk; indigo (a blue dye), wax and resin; slaves from Russia; wheat, wine, rice and caviar. The merchants deposited their wealth in the great bank of Genoa, the *Casa di San Giorgio*.

A busy street in Genoa. Below: the city in the fifteenth century, drawn by an artist of the time.

Learning to Sail

Despite the dangers of storms and pirates, the easiest and safest way to travel in the fifteenth century was by sea. Traders travelling by road had to contend with moors and forests, robbers and wild animals. Genoese ships regularly sailed out into the Atlantic through the Strait of Gibraltar. Portuguese sailors had explored the coast of Africa, and in 1487 Bartolomeo Diaz, a Portuguese captain, discovered the Cape of Good Hope.

By the fifteenth century sailors had precise charts showing correct distances and compass bearings. Dom Henrique, a Portuguese prince, had founded a School of Navigation at Sagres, and by the 1490s there were many skilled sailors who were able to travel across familiar waters using the sun and the stars for guidance.

Genoa was famous for its map-makers,

traders and explorers, so it is not surprising that many of the city's young men became sailors. Columbus wrote that he went to sea at the age of 14, although there are few records of the voyages that he made in his early years. There is some evidence to suggest that he might have sailed with a famous pirate called Columbo the Younger.

In 1476 a Genoese ship, on which Cristoforo was a sailor, was attacked off the coast of Portugal. Using an oar to help him stay afloat, Columbus managed to swim the 6 miles (10 kilometres) to Lisbon. There, he told the Portuguese that he was from a noble family ruined by war. He changed his name to Cristovão Colom and married the daughter of a Portuguese nobleman.

Young Genoese boys learn practical seamanship while making local trading and fishing trips along the coast. They learn to study the tides and weather, and to interpret signs such as floating plants and driftwood.

The Portuguese Experts

Columbus was not the first person to consider travelling to the East by sailing west round the back of the world. Two hundred years before Columbus, a Genoese merchant family, the Vivaldis, had tried unsuccessfully to sail 'to the regions of India by way of the Ocean Sea [the Atlantic]'.

In Portugal, Columbus taught himself astronomy and arithmetic, and read 'everything that has been written' on geography and history. On voyages to Africa, he realized that the lands beyond Europe were not uninhabitable. He sailed 'one hundred leagues' – more than 300 miles (480 kilometres) – beyond Iceland in 1477 and heard from other sailors of strange men who had been washed ashore in Ireland. In Madeira and the Canary Islands, he found unknown plants washed ashore from the west.

In 1481 he corresponded with an aged Italian scholar who had calculated that Cipangu (Japan) was only 3,500 miles (5,600 kilometres) away across the Atlantic. Columbus recalculated this figure to 2,750 miles (4,400 kilometres) and in 1484 he asked King João II of Portugal to finance an expedition to Japan. At that time Portugal was in the forefront of Atlantic exploration, so the king was the obvious person to ask for help.

A group of Portuguese experts in mathematics and geography have been called together by King João. They question Columbus, who explains his ideas to them, using dividers.

The coasts of Europe have been accurately mapped on portolans – the first sea charts. Beyond Europe, however, Columbus's charts are guesswork. He has made many mistakes and the experts, who know much more than he does, reject his calculations. They doubt that Japan exists, and think he is asking too great a reward for himself.

Japan is actually more than 12,000 miles (19,300 kilometres) to the west of Spain. It is sheer chance that the West Indies lie roughly where Columbus estimates Japan to be.

La Rábida

In 1485 Columbus left Portugal. His ideas had been rejected, his wife had died and he was faced with increasing debts. He fled to Spain with his young son, Diego. According to legend, he was so poor that he had to beg for bread and a cup of water from the monastery of La Rábida near the town of Palos.

In Spain, however, Columbus met Antonio de Marchena, an influential friar. Marchena arranged for him to meet King Fernando and Queen Isabela (Ferdinand and Isabella) of Spain in May 1486. Without this stroke of luck a poor commoner such as Columbus would never have had the opportunity to make a personal request to the sovereigns to pay for his expedition.

Some historians believe that the queen was fond of Columbus, but she nevertheless merely referred the matter to a commission led by one of her priests, Hernando de Talavera. For four years Cristóbal Colón, as the Spanish knew him, attended this commission, arguing with churchmen who quoted the Old Testament and the writings of St Augustine. Columbus was a self taught sailor, not a scholar, and the Spanish treated him with contempt. Meanwhile, he scraped a living by selling books. Sometimes he almost despaired.

In 1490 the Talavera commission reported that Columbus's ideas were 'vain and worthy of rejection'. It concluded that a voyage to Asia would take three years; that St Augustine had said there were no antipodes; that the places Columbus wanted to visit were uninhabitable, and that a ship which sailed there would never return.

In 1491 Columbus returns to La Rábida. One of the friars, Juan Pérez, introduces him to Dr Fernández, an astronomer, Pero Vásquez, an experienced navigator, and Martín Alonso Pinzón, a local merchant and sea captain. Watched by Diego, they help Columbus to rethink his arguments. In July 1491 the little group decides to approach the king and queen once again.

Encamped outside Granada

Queen Isabela is sometimes described as 'a model for teenage girls, women, mothers and heads of government'. Some people want to make her a saint of the Roman Catholic Church. At the same time she was a tough dictator, who set up an armed force called the *Santa Hermandad* to establish royal power.

Towards the end of the fifteenth century, many people turned to religion. They were afraid that the world was going to end in 1500. There were rumours that in Germany the rain had turned to blood, and that in Rome a bolt of lightning had thrown the Pope from his throne.

In Spain, Isabela and Fernando shared the religious devotion of the age. They introduced the Inquisition to hunt down non-Catholics. Isabela's confessor, Tomás de Torquemada, was put in charge of it and during his term of office more than 10,000 heretics (people with different beliefs) were burned at the stake.

In full armour, Isabela rode to war against the Muslim kingdom of Granada (its capital city was also called Granada). During her reign more than 150,000 Jews living in Spain were expelled. A Jewish historian has suggested that Columbus was a Jew, hoping to find a new world where the Jews could go to escape from Isabela.

Columbus, however, supported the queen's religious fanaticism. According to a writer of the time, he fought 'with distinguished bravery' at Granada, and offered to use the profits of his expedition for a crusade to recapture Jerusalem from the Muslims.

The sovereigns' conquest of Granada (January 1492) frees them to support Columbus. Kneeling before Isabela, he is appointed Admiral of the Ocean Sea and Governor of the Indies (the lands in the region of India). He is ordered to try to sail westwards to India, and is promised a tenth of the wealth of the lands he finds.

Equipping the First Voyage

Columbus, Admiral of the Ocean Sea, arrived back in Palos on 22 May 1492 with letters from Fernando and Isabela ordering the town to supply and equip ships for his voyage within ten days.

He met with a cool reception. According to an eye-witness, 'the inhabitants of Palos thought that anyone who sailed with Columbus was death-marked'. They complained about the trouble of organizing an expedition already rejected by the Portuguese. Columbus accused them of conspiracy and treachery.

Eventually, Martín Alonso Pinzón set about recruiting men for Columbus. It was said that 'for every man he had pleasant words and money; so that with this and the general trust in him, many people followed him'. After ten weeks, everything was ready for the expedition.

Columbus's world-changing fleet comprised three tiny ships, all smaller than 100 tons (a 100-ton ship could carry 100 tuns, or barrels, of wine). None of the ships was longer than 80 feet (24 metres). The *Niña* and the *Pinta* were caravels, the fast sturdy ships developed by the Portuguese for their voyages of exploration. To Columbus's annoyance, he could not hire a third caravel; instead, he had to take a *nao*, the *Santa María*, a heavy cargo ship that rolled around in the sea like a barrel.

Martín Alonso Pinzón, Columbus and the ship's chandler supervise the loading of food and equipment. The sovereigns are paying for the voyage, so careful records must be kept.

Palos is on Spain's Atlantic coast and many of the local seamen are experienced sailors. Some have gone on Portuguese expeditions out into the Ocean Sea. Others have sailed with the local fishing fleet, or accompanied slave traders along the coast of Africa.

On the Voyage

In Columbus's time the captain took respon-
sibility for the general running of the ship; the
pilot and master were in charge of navigation
and the crew.

The pilot 'logged' the ship's speed by drop-
ping a plank in the water and watching how
quickly the ship sailed past it. He recorded
the ship's direction, as shown on the compass,
by inserting a peg into a traverse board every
half hour. In this way, since he knew both direction and speed, he could mark the position

of the ship on a sheepskin chart by pricking
it with the points of dividers. This method of
navigation is called dead reckoning.

Columbus always underestimated distances.
He thought that if the crew found out how
far they had sailed, they would be overcome
with fear.

The boatswain looked after the sails and
anchors, and killed the rats. At night, he
extinguished the iron fire box in the galley,
which was used for cooking. The steward
supervised the food, water and wine. Below
deck, a caulker manned the pumps and tried
to stop the leaks. Three doctors, a cooper

(who mended the barrels) and a gunner also
sailed with the fleet.

The helmsman, who is in charge of the rudder, stands
in the afterdeck. He can see neither the sky nor the
sails, so the pilot or master shouts down instructions
from the deck. In heavy seas, up to a dozen men are
needed to control the rudder.

There are no clocks on board ship. Throughout
the day, a gromet (ordinary seaman) turns the half-
hour glass.

Right, clockwise: a half-hour glass, a compass, an
astrolabe (to calculate the ship's position using the
stars), a log book, quill pens, dividers and, in the
centre, a traverse board.

Life on Board

Each day was divided into six watches of four hours. The gromets were on duty every other watch. The first watch of the day began at 3 a.m., when a boy sang a short hymn, then said the Lord's Prayer and a short prayer for 'good days, good sailing and good company'.

At about 11 a.m. a gromet spread a cloth on deck and laid out some ship's biscuit and beef bones (full of maggots by the end of the voyage). There might also be some beans, dried meat or fish, and some wine. All the ship's company, saying 'Amen', immediately rushed out and devoured the food. 'It is like an antheap…the people around you will belch, or vomit, or break wind, or empty their bowels, while you are having your breakfast,' a traveller complained.

The afternoon watch (3-7 p.m.) was fairly easy. The men did routine maintenance, told tales and searched for lice in their clothes and hair, while the lookout kept watch from the crow's-nest. At sunset a boy sang a hymn called the *Salve Regina*.

Columbus had a cabin (see below) but the sailors slept on deck; the favourite place was the flat hatch cover. There was little furniture. A captain took three chests for his personal belongings; three gromets shared one chest. A precarious, wave-battered wooden seat hung out over the handrail served as the lavatory. In bad weather it was rarely used and human excrement collected in the hold.

Far right: a gromet climbs up the 'ratlines' to adjust the rigging and the sails.
Top right: examining the lead, a plumb-line used to test the depth of the water. Fat is smeared on the bottom to reveal the nature of the seabed; the sand, shells or stones stick to the fat. Centre right: the sailors' diet includes neither fresh fruit nor vegetables. Many men die of scurvy, a disease caused by lack of vitamin C. Below right: splicing, to join together two pieces of rope.

First Sighting

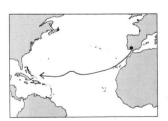

As the ships sailed further from Spain, Columbus's crew became so frightened that by 6 October they were openly threatening to throw him overboard and return home. Martín Alonso Pinzón on the *Pinta* sailed alongside the *Santa María* and shouted across loudly that he would hang the troublemakers if the Admiral wished. There was no more talk of mutiny.

There were a number of false sightings of land, but Columbus refused to turn off course to investigate any of them. Instead, he warned that anyone mistakenly crying 'Land!' would forfeit the generous prize of 10,000 maravedis offered for the first sighting.

On 11 October 1492 lookouts saw a carved stick and a twig covered in barnacles floating in the sea. It seemed that land was near, so Columbus doubled the number of lookouts, urging the men to be vigilant. He did not want his voyage to end in shipwreck on an unknown reef.

Standing on deck at about midnight, Columbus thought he saw a light 'like a little wax candle'. At 2 a.m. on 12 October gunfire from the *Pinta* told him land had been sighted.

Columbus anchored off one of a group of islands known today as the Bahamas. He went ashore, planted the royal banner, and took possession of it in the name of the King and Queen of Spain, naming two nearby islands Fernandina and Isabela after the sovereigns. Although he later called the lands he had discovered a *nuevo mundo* (new world), it is certain that Columbus thought he had discovered Cipangu (Japan) and the Indies in east Asia.

Historians disagree about which island Columbus discovered first. Columbus called it San Salvador, meaning Holy Saviour.

It is 2 a.m. on 12 October 1492. Rodrigo de Triana, the lookout on the *Pinta*, sights land. Columbus promises him a present but keeps the prize for himself, claiming that he had seen the fires of the island two hours earlier.

Strange Visitors

One day in October 1492 the inhabitants of a tiny island in the Bahamas discovered strangely dressed men coming ashore from a large wooden boat. They decided that they must be gods sent from heaven.

The Taino people who met Columbus lived a peaceful, unhurried life. Much of their leisure time was spent lying in *hamaca* (hammocks) smoking dried leaves through Y-shaped tubes called *tabaca*, while the older women told stories.

The old people cared for the children and prepared the meals. The Tainos ate sweet potatoes (called *batata*, from which comes our word 'potato') and cassava bread. The cassava root is poisonous, so it had to be pulped and strained before it could be eaten.

The young women cultivated the fields and the young men went hunting for snakes, turtles and iguanas, which were considered a great delicacy. The *guacicomo* (a species of fish with suckers round its mouth) was used to catch other fish. When it attached itself to its prey, the fishermen hauled them both in by means of a string fastened through its tail.

The Tainos worshipped a supreme god, but also believed in *zemis* (spirits). Some families kept the skull of an ancestor in a small wicker basket, thinking that this would protect them. Old women were thought to be able to invoke curses, and people with incurable diseases were buried before they had died, but Columbus was delighted by these friendly and gentle people. 'They love their neighbour as themselves...and always speak with a smile,' he wrote.

Led by their cacique (chief), the natives trade and exchange gifts. They are Lucayans of the Caribbean Taino culture, but, believing he is in Asia, Columbus calls them *Indios* (Indians). They welcome the Spaniards and Columbus thinks that '50 armed men will make them do everything we want'.

Shipwrecked at La Navidad

Columbus sailed from island to island, exploring the new lands he had found. On 22 November 1492 he was deserted by Martín Alonso Pinzón, who sailed off to look for an island of gold that the natives had told him about. 'It was a dirty trick,' Columbus wrote in his log. 'He has done and said many other bad things to me.'

On 6 December Columbus discovered Haiti and marvelled at its 'beauty and excellence'. It so reminded him of home that he named it La Isla Española (the Spanish island).

On Christmas Eve, 1492, Columbus set sail again, along the north coast of Española. He left the deck at 11 p.m. As soon as he had gone the helmsman slipped away to sleep, leaving only a young gromet to turn the glass and hold the tiller. As the boy turned the second half-hour of the watch, the ship ran aground.

Like most ships of the time, the *Santa María* was fastened together with wooden pegs. She literally fell apart and Columbus was forced to abandon ship. Helped by men from a village nearby, the crew salvaged what they could. The local cacique, who was called Guacangarí, gave his shipwrecked visitors two large houses in the centre of his village. He also gave them gold masks, jewellery and four gold nuggets 'as large as a man's hand'.

Columbus left thirty-nine of his men, including a doctor, a carpenter and a gunner, to establish a colony in this friendly place. Their orders were to build a fort from the timbers of the *Santa Maria*, and then to look for gold.

Spanish gunners give an artillery display to impress the Taino leaders. 'It is right', Columbus writes in his log, 'that the Indians may obey Your Highnesses with love and fear.'

Columbus calls the settlement La Navidad (Nativity) because the shipwreck occurred on Christmas Day.

Home to Palos

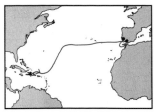

Taking six Tainos with him to show to King Fernando and Queen Isabela, Columbus set sail from La Navidad in the *Niña* on 4 January 1493. Two days later he met Martín Alonso Pinzón in the *Pinta* off the coast of Española. Columbus wrote that no harsh words were exchanged, in order 'to prevent Satan from hindering this voyage, as he has done up until now'. Back in La Navidad, the settlers had already stopped work on the fort, seeing little to fear from the Tainos.

The two ships sailed north and caught the westerly trade winds across the Atlantic. Columbus saw three mermaids (sea cows), but commented that he did not think they looked much like women. The ships sailed slowly, because the mast of the *Pinta* was weakened by rot and both vessels were suffering from shipworm. For three days (12-14 February) they endured a violent storm.

Columbus, however, survived the storm and reached Lisbon in Portugal on 4 March 1493. For a week he boasted about his achievement to King João II. He so infuriated the Portuguese courtiers that they almost assassinated him.

Finally, on Friday 15 March, the *Niña* entered Palos – followed, in the early evening of the same day, by the *Pinta*. She, too, had survived the storm, and had landed in northern Spain in late February. Her crew had been the first to sight the New World and the first back with the news. Martín Alonso Pinzón, however, was a sick man and he died a few days later.

As the storm drives the *Pinta* from view, the sailors on the *Niña* fear they will die, perhaps devoured by sea-monsters (see below).

Columbus is afraid that he will not survive to tell anybody about his voyage. However, when they draw lots to see who will go on pilgrimage if they are saved, Columbus chooses the marked bean.

Processions and Praise

Columbus rested for a fortnight at the monastery of La Rábida with Juan Pérez, then set off on the long journey to Barcelona to meet the sovereigns.

Columbus was not the first person to sail across the Atlantic, but the publicity he arranged for himself helped to assure his place in history. The six Tainos, painted and wearing their gold ornaments, led the procession, followed by men carrying parrots and strange, stuffed animals. Columbus followed on horseback, surrounded by a host of young noblemen begging to go on the next voyage. At every village the people turned out to stare and to cheer.

On 30 April 1493 Columbus arrived in Barcelona, where he received the highest honours. His food was tasted to make sure it was not poisoned and he rode in public next

to King Fernando, an honour previously given only to the king's son.

Many years later a story about Columbus became popular. Insulted at a feast by a man who told him that someone else would eventually have discovered the islands, Columbus invited the guests to balance an egg on its end. After they had all failed, he crushed the end and stood the egg on the table. 'Everything is easy', he told them, 'when someone has shown you what to do.'

The sovereigns receive Columbus as if he were a person of the highest rank. They forbid him to kneel to kiss their hands and invite him to sit in their presence.

Columbus speaks for an hour. He has been to Cipangu (Japan), he says, and has brought back gold and jewellery – a sample, he claims, of the wealth of this land, where the rivers run with gold. He calls the Tainos out from behind a screen and speaks of their gentleness and their willingness to receive the Roman Catholic faith.

While the choir sings a *Te Deum*, Fernando and Isabela fall to their knees in tears and thank God.

Pilgrimage and Prayers

Like many men in Renaissance times, Columbus was proud, complaining, greedy – and very religious.

Now, out of the profits he expected to make from his discoveries, he promised to provide an army of 4,000 cavalrymen and 50,000 footsoldiers to recapture the Holy Sepulchre at Jerusalem. The Tainos he had brought to Spain were baptized on his orders. He changed his signature again, this time to Christoferens – for he was 'the bearer of Christ' to the people of the new islands. 'I knew that they were a people to be delivered to our holy faith rather by love than by force,' he wrote.

Fernando and Isabela did not, as some historians have suggested, secretly laugh at Columbus's faith. They gave orders for a new expedition, the first task of which was to be the conversion of the natives. Bernardo Buil, a Benedictine monk, and five priests were to go with the fleet to accomplish this, and Columbus was instructed to treat the Indians 'very well and lovingly'.

Above: Columbus's new signature. The three Greek letters at the start of his name stand for 'Christo'. It is not known what the letters above his name mean, but scholars believe they denote some religious phrase such as 'I am the servant of the Most High'.

Right: kneeling at the shrine of Our Lady in the Spanish village of Guadalupe, Columbus gives thanks – as he had promised – for safe deliverance from the storm (see page 32). He promises the monks of Guadalupe that on his next voyage he will name an island after their village.

To Columbus, his success is certain proof that God 'grants to all who walk in His way victory over apparent impossibilities'.

Exploiting the New World

The printing press had been invented in about 1450, so news of Columbus's achievement gradually spread – to Italy and England during 1493, to France by 1494 and to Germany by 1497. Unlike the Vikings or Marco Polo, Columbus lived at a time when there were many merchants eager to hear about new trading opportunities and to take advantage of them. That is why Columbus's voyages of discovery changed the world.

At first, trade with the Americas – controlled after 1503 by the *Casa de Contratación* in Spain – brought only luxuries to Europe for the use of the rich: pearls from Venezuela and brazil wood (from which a red dye was made) from Brazil. Before long, however, even ordinary people's lives began to be changed by the imports from the New World. Columbus had brought back ears of maize from his first voyage. By the end of the sixteenth century, maize – and the potato, introduced from Peru – were common in western Europe, and the fashion-conscious took snuff, chewed tobacco as a medicine and drank chocolate sweetened with sugar.

The colonists of the New World relied on Europe for all the finer things of life – wine, glass and books – and many everyday essentials such as weapons, clothing, wheat and household utensils. The first slaves were taken to the New World in 1502.

In return, dozens of ships (over 60 a year by 1550) sailing in convoy to avoid pirates, brought vast amounts of gold and silver back to Spain from Mexico and Peru. For a while Spain became the richest nation on earth.

The produce of the New World (clockwise, from top): yams, sugar cane, sweet potatoes, cassava root, cocoa beans, guavas, ginger, peppers, gold, maize, cotton and brazil wood. Centre: tobacco leaves and papayas.

The Third Voyage

On 30 May 1498 Columbus set sail for America again with six ships. He wanted to investigate reports of a great continent to the south of the Indies, as it was generally thought that 'precious things come from very hot regions where the inhabitants are black'.

During the voyage, however, the fleet was becalmed in the doldrums where there is little wind, and the ships drifted under a blazing sun. 'The casks of wine and water burst. The wheat burnt like fire; the salt pork scorched and went bad,' wrote Columbus, perhaps with some exaggeration because he was ill during the voyage.

On 31 July, with only one barrel of fresh water left, Columbus saw the summits of three mountains on the horizon. Thanking God the Father, Son and Holy Spirit for his deliverance, he named the island after the Holy Trinity – La Trinidad.

Sailing south of the island, he landed on the Paria peninsula of South America on 5 August 1498. Columbus noticed that the water was fresh for 72 miles (115 kilometres) from the shore, evidence of a huge river (the Orinoco) flowing into the sea. 'This land is a great continent, unknown until now,' he deduced. He was the first European to stand on the South American mainland.

Columbus calculates latitude using the height of the stars above the horizon (the angle of altitude); since the earth's surface is curved, this appears to change according to the latitude of the observer. He uses a quadrant (see also below) to measure the angle of altitude, which a gromet reads off the scale on the bottom.

Sometimes a navigator might use a cross-staff (above), adjusting the transom (cross-piece) to find out the height of the star.

Columbus had noticed that magnetic north – the direction in which the compass needle points – changed as he crossed the Atlantic. On Paria he checks his calculations, with the same result. He decides that the earth 'is not a true sphere, as scholars have told us, but like a pear' and that he is now near 'the stalk, where it sticks out'. On top of this mountain, he writes, is the Earthly Paradise, the Garden of Eden.

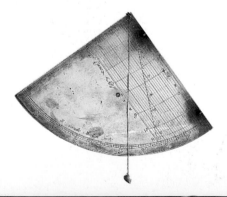

Rebellion and Imprisonment

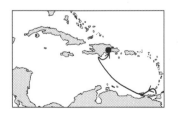

Columbus was ill. His eyes were so sore that they bled. In mid-August 1498 he called off his explorations around the Paria peninsula and sailed to Española.

While Columbus had been in Spain, his two brothers Bartolomeo and Diego had moved the colonists' settlement from Isabela to a healthier site on the south coast of Española. They had called it Santo Domingo, after their father, Domenico. Conditions on Española had improved a little. The colony was producing its own bread, pork and beef. In October a boatload of Taino slaves and brazil wood was sent back to Spain.

Columbus had, however, to report that the Taino caciques were still at war with the Spanish settlers, and that many colonists, also, were in open revolt. The rebellion was led by

Francisco Roldán, the *alcalde* (magistrate) of the settlement. When Columbus made peace with Roldán, the *alcalde* promptly caused another rebellion by imprisoning a settler who had kidnapped his Taino woman. This new rebellion was defeated and its leader, Adrian de Moxica, was imprisoned. When he refused to say confession to a priest, Columbus had him thrown from the prison walls.

Back in Spain angry colonists told Fernando and Isabela that Columbus was a cruel man, a 'shedder of Spanish blood', who planned to seize Española and make himself king of the New World. In 1500 a Spanish nobleman, Francisco de Bobadilla, was sent to see what was going on. He took evidence from everybody who hated the Admiral, arrested the three Columbus brothers and sent them back to Spain in chains.

Columbus's men have overcome a small group of rebels – many of them criminals allowed to come to Española as an alternative to execution. The defeated rebels are hanged on the spot.

Columbus in Chains

Having docked at Cadiz in October 1500, Columbus went to stay at the monastery of Las Cuevas in Seville. He was still in chains and accompanied by his jailer.

'I have made a new voyage, to a new heaven and a new earth, and made Spain the wealthiest of countries,' he complained, 'yet I am treated as if I had stolen the Indies. Who would believe such a thing?'

While Columbus was at Las Cuevas he rested and prayed. He also wrote two books. *The Book of Privileges* was a collection of all the documents in which the sovereigns had promised him his rights and titles. *The Book of Prophecies* included a number of biblical passages which he used to support his argument that he had been chosen by God to discover the route to the Indies.

After keeping him waiting for two months, the sovereigns received Columbus at court. His chains were removed, but ever after he kept them in his bedroom, to remind him of how he had been rewarded for his services.

Columbus was not, however, sent back to Española. Instead, in September 1501, Nicolás de Ovando, one of Fernando's favourites, was appointed Governor of the Indies. Ovando set sail in February 1502 with 30 ships and 2,500 men.

Eventually, on 14 March 1502, Fernando and Isabela authorized Columbus's fourth and final voyage to the New World. He was instructed to sail west again, to try to find a new route to India across the Ocean Sea. If he succeeded, he would be able to sail around the world.

On his way to meet Fernando and Isabela in December 1500, Columbus refuses to remove his shackles. He has been put in chains in the sovereigns' names, he says, and only the sovereigns can remove them.

When crowds along the route see how he has been treated, there is a public outcry. To ordinary people, he is still a hero.

The Fourth Voyage

Columbus was 51 years old when, on 9 May 1502, he set out from Cadiz with four ships on his fourth voyage. With him went his 12-year-old son Fernando (who wrote an account of the voyage) and, under protest, his brother Bartolomeo. The crew was cobbled together from old friends from past voyages and young lads out for adventure – 56 ship's boys and 43 ordinary seamen.

The ships had an easy voyage to the Indies, arriving at Matininó (Martinique) on 15 June. Columbus refilled the water casks and made the men wash their clothes. Then, against the sovereigns' clear orders, he sailed to Española. He wanted, wrote his son Fernando, to try to exchange one of his ships, the *Santiago*, which was 'a crank and a dull sailer', for a better vessel. In addition, he had noticed a number of dolphins and seals, and sensed from these signs that a storm was about to break.

At Santo Domingo, however, Nicolás de Ovando refused to allow Columbus to enter the harbour. The new governor had spent three months on Española sorting out the problems Columbus had been unable to solve. Bobadilla was about to return to Spain with a fleet of 28 ships, a large amount of gold and most of the rebels, and Ovando did not want Columbus causing trouble.

As to the storm, the Spaniards in Santo Domingo openly mocked the Admiral as 'a prophet and a fortune-teller'. While Columbus found shelter in a nearby bay, Bobadilla's fleet set sail for Spain.

Before Columbus sets off on his fourth voyage (see map, above) he refits his ships. After the barnacles have been scraped off the bottom, his men repair the caulking (waterproofing), using a hemp rope and tar. The hull will then be covered with tallow (animal fat).

Seeking a West Passage

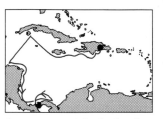

On 30 June 1502 the storm struck. Bobadilla and the rebels drowned and 24 ships sank immediately. Columbus, however, safe in harbour, survived the storm and sailed westwards, exploring the coast of Central America (see map, inset). He hoped to find a westward passage to India.

The native inhabitants on the mainland had expertly woven cotton shawls and could work copper, but they were 'painted like devils' and thought the Spaniards were trying to bewitch them. On 17 October, at Guayga, they attacked the ships, blowing horns and spitting at the Spaniards (a type of curse). On 9 November, when Columbus tried to capture some of them, they swam away from his boats, diving like sea birds to escape capture. 'It was really funny to see the

boats chasing them and the rowers wearing themselves out in vain,' Columbus's son Fernando wrote.

The bad weather returned. Columbus became ill with gout. Finally, on 6 January 1503, he moored in the mouth of a river which he called the Belén (Bethlehem), and built a small settlement. It rained ceaselessly until 14 February and the ships became trapped by a sandbank which formed in the river mouth. The inhabitants of this country, which Columbus called Veragua (present-day Panama), told him that there was sea on both sides of this land and that it was only ten days' sail to India. Columbus was only a few miles from the Pacific Ocean, but he was thousands of miles away from the passage to India.

The Taínos of Española call the storm a *huracán*. The only ship which manages to continue to Spain safely is the one carrying Columbus's share of the gold mined in the past year. To Columbus, the storm is God's judgement. To his enemies, it seems like witchcraft.

Jamaica Moon

In March 1503 Columbus learned that the *Quibian* (local chief) intended to kill them all, so he abandoned the settlement in Veragua and set sail for Española.

By this time, however, 'all the people, with pumps, kettles and pans were not enough to bail out the water that entered by the wormholes', young Fernando remembered. One ship sank and the two that remained staggered to Jamaica. On 25 June the men ran them aground, fortified them against attack and used palm leaves to make rough shelters on the decks.

There was no hope that they would be rescued by a passing ship. Columbus bought two Taino canoes and ordered Diego Méndez, his chief clerk, and Bartolomeo Fieschi, a sailor from Genoa, to paddle to Española –

a journey of more than 100 miles (160 kilo-metres). Then he waited, trading hawks' bells and sailors' caps for cassava bread and meat.

Columbus was tested to the full during the following year. By February the Tainos had tired of trading food for trinkets. Columbus, who had been waiting for an eclipse of the moon on 29 February (to make an accurate calculation of latitude) told them that God would darken the moon unless they provided food. That night, as the shadow of the eclipse darkened the moon, the Tainos hurried to the ships with food, begging Columbus to pray to his God to save them.

Columbus also had to face a mutiny. In a pitched battle on 19 May 1504, watched by the bewildered Tainos, Columbus's brother Bartolomeo killed a number of the rebels and took their leader prisoner.

It is March 1504. Many months have passed, yet there is no sign of Méndez and Fieschi. Unknown to Columbus, although they have reached Española, the Governor is in no hurry to rescue the Admiral.

An End and a Beginning

In June 1504, one year after they had been marooned, the rescue ship arrived, and on 13 August Columbus sailed into Santo Domingo, which was already quite a thriving town. Ovando, the Governor, greeted him with a show of affection. It was, young Fernando wrote, 'the kiss of a scorpion'.

When Columbus returned to Spain in November, he was too ill to travel any more. He rented a house in Seville and spent his time petitioning the sovereigns. He wanted them to give him, as they had promised, a tenth of the revenues of the mines of Española. Even though they allowed him only a fiftieth of the gold, he still became a rich man.

Columbus died on 20 May 1506. His son Diego married into the royal family and in 1509 went to Española as Admiral of the Ocean Sea and Governor of the Indies.

Columbus never went to North America, and thought that he had found Japan and the Indies. He boasted and exaggerated, yet never succeeded in controlling the colony of which he was governor. His discoveries brought about the annihilation of the Taino people and their civilization.

Yet Columbus's story is truly incredible. The son of an obscure Italian weaver, he captained the first expedition to the New World. He was the first European in the Caribbean and the first to reach South America. Time after time he escaped death from shipwreck, rebellion and disease. His voyages changed the course of history. 'To Spain', claimed a sixteenth-century writer, 'Columbus gave a New World. History knows of no man who ever did the like.'

On 12 September 1504 Columbus leaves Santo Domingo for Spain. Crippled with gout, he is helped down to the shore. He knows that he will never return.

How Do We Know?

There are many sources for the historian who wants to find out about Columbus, but it is important to know who is writing, when and why. These things determine to what extent you can rely on the truthfulness of the source.

Personal accounts

Columbus kept a record of his voyages. Although the original log books have been lost, Bartolomé de Las Casas, the son of one of Columbus's men, copied the logs written during the first and third voyages, adding his own notes. Las Casas changed Columbus's text, but it is not known how much he changed it – did he just correct the grammar, or alter whole passages? Las Casas generally supported Columbus, so it is not surprising that Columbus emerges as calm and masterful.

The log of the second voyage has disappeared. For evidence, we have to rely mainly on three accounts written by members of the crew. In these sources Columbus does not appear quite as good a leader as he did on the first voyage. In addition, one of the writers, Diego Chanca, the surgeon, was prejudiced against the native peoples and it is he who includes evidence about the cannibalism of the Caribs. Historians feel this was exaggerated by the Spanish settlers, to excuse the atrocities they committed.

Columbus never wrote an autobiography, but *The Book of Privileges* (see above right) and *The Book of Prophecies* which he wrote in 1500 (see page 53) have survived, along with many of his letters. In addition, Columbus's son Fernando wrote a biography of his father, although he was constantly trying to show that Columbus was in the right. For example, the only surviving account of the report of the Talavera commission (see page 15) appears in his book. It is unlikely, however, that a large commission of learned men would come to conclusions quite as foolish as those that Fernando reports. Fernando sailed on the fourth voyage, and it is interesting to compare his account with a letter which Columbus sent to the King and Queen of Spain about the voyage. Columbus is full of gloom, but Fernando's story is full of adventure and fun, as you would expect from someone who saw events through the eyes of a teenager.

After Columbus's death, his family tried to obtain the money due to him from the Spanish government, and a number of court cases were held. The statements made at these hearings are called *pleitos*. Historians have to remember, however, that they were all biased and made about 20 years after the events.

Research

We will never know what the Tainos thought or were really like because they left no writings, and the Spaniards destroyed their treasures and possessions. Historians have to rely on descriptions written by Spanish settlers, many of whom did not understand the native culture. A few Arawak Tainos still live in South America, but they may no longer have the same life style and beliefs.

No one knows what Columbus looked like, because his portrait was not painted during his lifetime. Nor is it known what his ships looked like, because they have rotted –

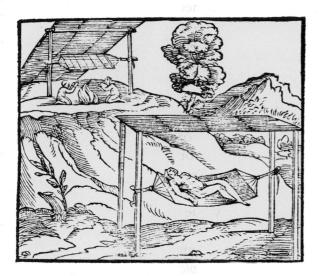

although historians make expert guesses based on ships of the time and clues in the log books.

Dedicated researchers, however, continue to turn up new facts about Columbus. One of the greatest was Alice B. Gould, who spent over twenty years (1924-44) searching through the Spanish archives, tracking down the names of 87 of the 90 men who sailed on the first voyage.

Columbus's early life is obscure, and for many years historians thought the *mayorazgo* (a document in which Columbus says he was born in Genoa) was a fake – the original was missing. During the Napoleonic Wars (1803–1815) the documents in the Spanish archives had been used as bedding for cavalry horses. Alice Gould sorted through hundreds of papers covered with dried manure until she found the original *mayorazgo*.

Archaeology can also answer some of the historian's questions. For example, until recently it was believed that Columbus's fort at La Navidad (see page 30) was built beside the sea, but archaeologists have discovered that not only was it sited inland, in the middle of a Taino village, but also that it was never finished. In a nearby well were found the remains of a European pig and a rat's tooth – there were no rats in the New World before Columbus's voyages.

Stories and misconceptions

Columbus was a controversial man and many stories and misconceptions have grown up about him. One of the most famous is the story about the egg (see page 35). Opponents of Columbus spread rumours to harm his reputation; one story claimed that he had been told about the New World by an 'unknown navigator' who had discovered America by accident.

Even modern historians have found it hard to write about Columbus without adding their prejudices and reminiscences about their own voyages. He has been criticized for being too religious, and for obsessively seeking power and gold at the expense of the native inhabitants. It has been suggested that, in this way, Columbus 'set the pattern' for the way the New World was settled and was therefore to blame for the atrocities of the next four centuries. In fact, Columbus spent much of his time trying to prevent others from harming the Tainos, and he cannot be blamed if he did not have a twentieth-century attitude to religion and native culture.

Columbus knew that people were criticizing him. In a letter describing the fourth voyage, he wrote about 'those who find fault, saying "Why did you not do something else?"'

His answer was simple. 'I should have liked', he wrote, 'to see *them* on this voyage.'

Index

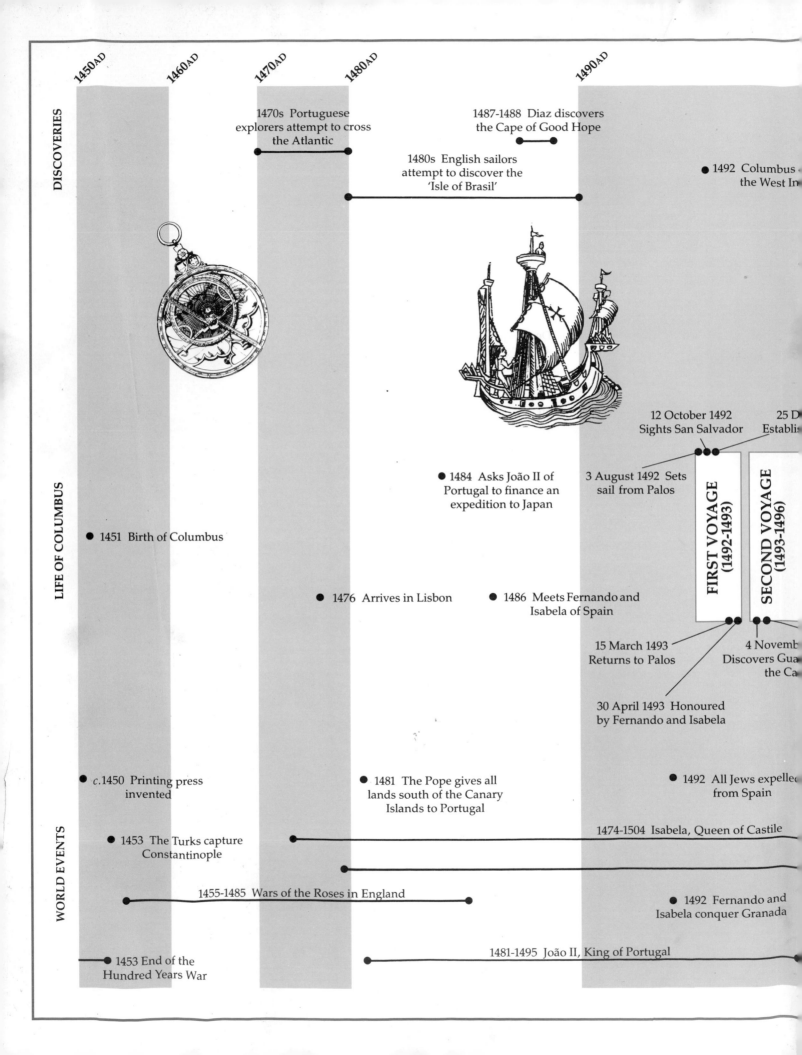

DISCOVERIES

1450AD   **1460**AD   **1470**AD   **1480**AD   **1490**AD

1470s Portuguese explorers attempt to cross the Atlantic

1487-1488 Diaz discovers the Cape of Good Hope

1480s English sailors attempt to discover the 'Isle of Brasil'

1492 Columbus the West In

LIFE OF COLUMBUS

12 October 1492 Sights San Salvador

25 D Establis

3 August 1492 Sets sail from Palos

1484 Asks João II of Portugal to finance an expedition to Japan

1451 Birth of Columbus

FIRST VOYAGE (1492-1493)

SECOND VOYAGE (1493-1496)

1476 Arrives in Lisbon

1486 Meets Fernando and Isabela of Spain

15 March 1493 Returns to Palos

4 Novemb Discovers Gua the Ca

30 April 1493 Honoured by Fernando and Isabela

c.1450 Printing press invented

1481 The Pope gives all lands south of the Canary Islands to Portugal

1492 All Jews expelle from Spain

1453 The Turks capture Constantinople

1474-1504 Isabela, Queen of Castile

1455-1485 Wars of the Roses in England

1492 Fernando and Isabela conquer Granada

WORLD EVENTS

1481-1495 João II, King of Portugal

1453 End of the Hundred Years War